Penny, Polly, and Peter Pig were planning a picnic. "What shall we pack in our picnic basket?" asked Penny.

Peter looked in the pantry.

"Let's pack some peaches," said Peter.

"A peachy idea!" said Polly.

"Are they ripe?" asked Penny.

"Perhaps we should taste them first," said Polly.

And they did.
"Perfect!" said Penny.

"Let's pack pickles," said Peter.
"Perhaps we should taste the pickles, too,"
said Polly.

4

And they did.
"MMMMMMM. Pickle-icious!" said Peter.

Peter made some peanut butter
and potato chip sandwiches.
"Would you like to taste them?"
Peter asked Penny and Polly.

"Yes, please!" said Penny and Polly.
And they did.

"Perhaps we should pack some pasta salad,"
said Polly.
"And pears and plums," said Penny.

"And pumpkin pie," said Peter.
Of course, Penny, Polly, and Peter
tasted everything first.

Before long, the pantry was empty.
But so was the picnic basket!
Penny, Polly, and Peter were puzzled.

"That's peculiar!" said Peter.

"I guess we'll have to put off our picnic," said Polly.

"We could order pizza instead," said Penny.

And they did!

How many things can you find that begin with the letter P?

See inside back cover for answers.

Pp Cheer

P is for pig, pickles, and pot

P is for pizza, gooey and hot

P is for pancakes, piled up high

P is for puppy, popcorn, and pie

Hooray for **P**, big and small—

the peachiest, peppiest letter of all!